Complete List of Elements
Of Self-Publishing
on Amazon and Other Online Booksellers

The Most Important Factors of Successfully Self-Publishing,
Marketing and Selling Your Print and eBook Online

Gürhan Demirkan

Published by

Cosmo
Publishing
Company

Cosmo Publishing Company - USA
(www.cosmopublishing.com)

Yazardan Direkt - Turkey
(www.yazardandirekt.com)

ISBN: 978-1-949872-00-2

Preface – Note to the Self-Publishing Authors

I have been helping authors publish and market their books for about twenty years. I've established an Internet marketing company and a publishing company in the United States, plus a second publishing company in Turkey, where I've been involved in both traditional and self-publishing as well as global Internet marketing.

In my experience, the elements of successful publishing don't change much, regardless of where and how you choose to publish. The bottom line is that you cannot, must not, should not ignore two fundamental factors:

Editing
Marketing & Advertising

This doesn't mean that you, as an author, should undermine or avoid dealing with other factors. Publishing your book and becoming a successful author require paying attention to the many intricacies of the business. But everything always comes down to one factor: *you — the author!*

This is the reason I wrote this book, to provide some valuable information regarding the elements of self-publishing. New authors in particular need to understand what's involved in this business at the most basic level, and what steps are required to find success.

Thank you for your interest in my small book. I hope you'll find all the success in world!

Gürhan Demirkan
Partner - Cosmo Publishing – USA & Partner - Yazardan Direkt – Turkey

Warning & Disclaimer

There is simply no reasonable way of including in this book all the information you might need on Self-Publishing and Book Marketing & Advertising, even if it were a thick manual.

The information I've provided in this book is up to date as of April 2018. But as everyone knows, information, websites, rules and regulations change at lightning speed these days. I'd appreciate your input. To offer any updates or suggestions, please send your feedback through our website at this page:

http://cosmopublishing.com/contact-cosmo-publishing/

Please also note: self-publishing is not a get-rich-quick scheme. Like any successful business, it requires long hours, hard work, information overload, lots of decision making, and—you guessed it! —investment!

Even though no one can guarantee your success, you should keep in mind that there are many self-publishing authors making an excellent living from their craft.

One more important note: The purpose of this book is to relay information to educate and entertain. I, Cosmo Publishing Company, and Yazardan Direkt shall bear neither liability nor responsibility to any person or entity with respect to any loss or damage caused, or alleged to have been caused, directly or indirectly, by the information contained in this book.

If you don't wish to be bound by the above, you may return this book to the publisher for a full refund.

What is Classic/Traditional Publishing, and How Does It Work?

Let's start by explaining that publishing, whether via a traditional publisher or self-publishing, starts with the author and ends with the author. The whole idea behind all publishing practices is to be fair to the author as well as the publishing house. In other words, there is no such thing as a fair or unfair, good or bad, way of publishing. It all depends on the method that works for you and for the publishing house.

It is simply a matter of choosing the most suitable method for yourself.

The industry is still developing, and new methods of publishing are coming to the market, especially the way the Internet is progressing. Nevertheless, if we consider the classic publishing _in the most traditional sense_, it works this way: an author writes his or her manuscript and submits it to the publisher, and the publisher purchases rights to the manuscript from the author. This type of publishing usually involves an advance payment to the author, plus a percentage from sales of the book in the future. When the book goes out for sale, the publisher gets reimbursed first from the sales of the book, until the advance payment is fully recovered. The author starts receiving royalties after the publishing house is fully compensated for the advance payment.

During the process of preparing the book for market (editing, cover design, and so on, which we will cover in the next chapters), the author does not pay for anything. Furthermore, distribution, marketing and advertising, which are definitely the most important aspects of publishing a book, also belong to the publisher. All this cost is absorbed by the publishing house.

In other words, the publishing house invests in the author and the manuscript in hopes that this investment will pay off with a profit. This is one of the main reasons publishing companies reject most manuscripts they receive. Since they are taking the risk of investing heavily in the author and manuscript, they must pick the best of the best to make sure they get their investment back - and make a profit on top of that.

Traditional publishing may vary from one deal to another, or from one author to another. Nevertheless, the fundamentals remain the same:

- The publishing house purchases rights to the manuscript for five years or more.
- An advance payment may be made to the author (though not always).
- The deal involves a percentage of the sales to the author, plus royalties.
- The publishing house absorbs all the costs associated with preparing the book for market, distribution, marketing, and advertising.
- The author pays none of these costs.
- The publishing house invests in the author and the manuscript.
- The publishing house gets first revenues from sales of the book until all costs associated with the book have been recovered, especially the advance payment to the author.
- Once the publishing house fully recovers its investment, it starts paying royalties to the author.

What is Self-Publishing?

Even though the process of self-publishing also starts with the author, it is a little different from traditional publishing. This time, the author becomes, in effect, the publishing house, taking charge of preparing the book for market (editing, cover, interior layout, etc.) as well as distribution, marketing and advertising.

In other words, self-publishing starts with the author, continues with the author, and ends, if at all, with the author.

So, the question is: Why go through all this trouble?

Each author may have his/her own reasons, but the most common ones are, first, a desire to retain all rights, and second, the fact that publishers reject all but a small percentage of the books submitted to them.

Before we get into a comparison of publishing methods, let's take a look at the main elements of publishing, to get a better understanding of the work involved in preparing a book for market, getting it distributed, and of course, the most important part of it; marketing and advertising.

Main Elements of Publishing

Since the purpose of this small book is to provide some broad information on Self-Publishing, we'll mention just the main elements, without going into great depth on every single one.

But we would like to make it (very) clear that among all the elements, these are the most important parts of the publishing business: Editorial, and Marketing & Advertising (M&A).

Having said that, let's start!

Editorial Services

My first recommendation would be to get yourself an editor. My second recommendation would be to get yourself an editor who syncs well with you. Yes, that is easier said than done, but this is vital for your writing career.

Before we get into explanations of various editorial services, you need to understand that they often overlap, and this is the main reason people are often confused about which one to select. Nevertheless, keep in mind that they are different services, which are needed at different stages of your writing process.

Here are the editorial services that you are going to deal with:

- Line Editing

    Your manuscript is complete; you've checked it once or twice and are feeling confident with it. Before you get into combing your manuscript for technical errors in grammar, hyphenation, etc., you may want to have someone check whether your manuscript actually communicates correctly to your readers with the language you are using. In other words, you want to know if your choice of words fluidly conveys the emotions, the information, and the sense of what you are trying to convey.
    - Can the dialogue be tightened?
    - Are you repeating the same material in different ways?
    - Are you digressing, phasing in and out of the subject from time to time?

- Are there perhaps clearer words you can use to explain or express your point of view?
- Are the structure of your sentences correct (verb tenses, etc.)
- Have you provided the right amount of detail in your scenes to help readers understand and be captivated?

Rather than zeroing in on the technical details of your manuscript, line editing is to improve the overall quality of your book, and in turn it is also a good way for you to improve your writing to become a better author.

- Copy

Now the technical corrections... and then some!

- Editing

On the technical side, this editing service deals with spelling, grammar, syntax, punctuation, capitalization, hyphenation, and fonts. The editor may also point out places where factual statements are incorrect.

Furthermore, copy editing also deals with inconsistencies in your writing. For example; On page 53, George goes into the bar with his dark black, mirrored shades on. Yet after the bar fight on page 65, he leaves the bar wearing his cool, brown shades.

In the publishing world, the copy editor always follows the line editor. In other words, the line editor helps you tell a better story, while the copy editor makes sure all the technical aspects of your story are correct.

- Proofreading (The Final Polish)

Your manuscript went through line editing, and then copy editing. Everything is complete as to the graphics, tables, layout, page numbers, etc. Now, you're thinking, it's time to get it to the press to have it printed. Not so fast! There is a person called proofreader who goes through your manuscript for a quality check, as in "final polish." His or her job is not to check on the work of any of the previous editors. The proofreader checks for consistency and accuracy in the text (spelling, hyphenation, etc.), and sometimes the layout, as well as the consistency and accuracy of the images.

As a side note, proofreaders have to know different styles, depending on the manuscript, for example Chicago Manual of Style, AP Style, The Elements Style.

- Editorial Evaluation

The Editorial Evaluation will give you an honest assessment of the marketability of your manuscript, and how much editing will be required. When you have invested hundreds of hours of your time in your manuscript and are getting ready to invest hundreds or maybe thousands of dollars of your money, editorial evaluation will be a fraction of that cost to give an appraisal of the following;

- How much work will be required to get your manuscript to the market
- How much editing is required of your manuscript
- Is your research sufficient for the subject of your manuscript?
- Quality of your sentence structure and word choice
- In the editorial evaluation, an experienced editor will give you constructive comments about issues such as overall structure, plot and character development, tone and audience, an overview of your manuscript, and an honest opinion as to whether your manuscript is market-ready

In other words, it is a cost-effective way of determining if your manuscript is marketable, and how much work is required to get it market-ready.

- ## Cover Copy Polish

  Anything that helps you sell your book, right? Well, this is one of the major ones, and your cover copy has to be written with one thing in mind: sales!

  What does that entail? Actually, more than you'd think. This is not just a text in which you talk about your book anymore. It goes beyond! Now you'll need to include your keywords (this will be covered in SEO—Search Engine Optimization), and you'll have to know your target audience to be able to appeal to their interests.

  If you can combine all that, all you need is an editor to go over your text to make sure everything works. If not, you need a copywriter, who has to know your book, understand your target audience, and be professionally capable of implementing your keywords in your cover copy.

Design Services

You can go way out of your way and spend a good bit of money on this, or you can pinch pennies. Which is best for you? The answer is: both can be, or neither. The point is not how much you spend, it is how well-targeted your spending is.

As was mentioned above when speaking about cover copy, it's all about knowing your target audience!

For example: is your audience teenagers or adults, males or females? What about their age and income? And more!

Since the purpose of this booklet is not to go into depth on the details of each aspect of publishing, we are only going to list services related to each category. But you should keep in mind that success lies in figuring out what will appeal to your target audience, not how pretty or beautiful it looks to you.

For example; if your target audience would prefer reading expensive-looking books with lavish interior and cover de-signs, then so be it. But if your readers would prefer plain, to-the-point, simple books, then that's the route you should take.

In other words, be mindful of your target audience before you start spending your money on these services.

- Interior Page Layout

Most people think this is related to elements such as font, pictures, illustrations, and tables included in the book. But in reality, it is much more. Here are couple of very basic pointers to begin with, just on page number-ing;

o There are some pages that should never have page numbers (pages with no text, for example), while others must have page numbers,
o Odd-numbered pages should always be on the right, even-numbered pages on the left.

Of course there are many more factors you need to con-sider, such as:

o Is the manuscript going to be an e-book, or printed?
o What is the genre (cookbook, novel, children's book, etc.?)
o The physical size of your book
o … and many more!

Your book is lot more than just a Microsoft Word® document; it requires detailed knowledge to get the interior layout done. In other words, you need to pre-pare a professional-looking book designed to suit your readers.

- Cover Design

"Don't judge a book by its cover." Maybe… but we also have to accept the fact that we are living in a digital world now, and that digital world is mostly visual. So, we have to have a great-looking cover.

And again, what exactly does that mean?

We repeatedly stress knowing your "target audi-ence," and this is another place where this is important. Why? Because it goes back to spending your hard-earned money wisely.

Be mindful of your audience, know your audience, know what they want to see and read! Is your audience looking for an intense-looking cover that may cost a lot? If yes, by all means then, get it done… but don't go out of your way paying a lot of money for a cover that's a lot more than your audience is looking for.

Another matter you should pay attention to is that most book sales now are accomplished with the buyer seeing nothing more than a thumbnail-size picture on the web. Keep this in mind when getting your book cover designed, as it has to convey the message and capture attention in a miniature size.

Book Formats

It is no secret that the major formats are:

- Print Books (since 1455!)

  A whole new era began when Johann Gutenberg mass-printed the first Bible. We now have books in many different sizes, quite a few different paper qualities, and lots of different paper colors. Nevertheless, even though you have many options for your book at any printer, the fact is that keeping the format and purchase price attractive to buyers will limit your choices. (This is the distribution side of your book, which we will touch on below.)

- e-Books (Kindle and ePub, and some iBooks)

  E-books are digital formats of your manuscript. There are quite a few different formats, but the major ones are the Kindle, which is the Amazon format, and ePub, which is widely accepted throughout the world. (And yes, there are more. But we are only going to cover a couple of them for the purpose of this booklet.)

  Let's make one thing clear: PDF is not an e-book format!

  There is plenty of information on the web as to how to convert your Microsoft Word manuscript into e-book format. At the same time, experts offer this service from as low as $50 to $300 or $400.

How do you know what is expensive and what is not? Unfortunately, there is no base price for this service. But the following points may help you understand what drives the cost of converting your book:

o The type of e-format you are looking for: reflowable, fixed layout, ePDF (which is not an ebook format, as mentioned above). Please keep in mind, the format you need to use may not always be related to the money that you are willing to spend. You may be stuck with a particular format for the type of e-book you are publishing (fixed layout for large illustrations and large text, reflowable for a regular book, and ePDF if you want to prevent yourself from selling your book with most retailers).
o Pictures, illustrations, tables: these require extra efforts, so the more of these you have, the more expensive your e-book will be.
o Your layout: the more elaborate the layout, the costlier the e-book.

- AudioBooks

Yes, there is a rising trend in sales and interest in audio formats, but making a professional audiobook is a little costly. You can hire a professional voice-over person, or even multiple people, to have your characters come alive with different personalities.

Here are some places where you can sell your audiobook:

- o Audible.com
- o Scribd.com
- o Downpour.com
- o Google Play Books (not necessarily audiobooks, whereby an app reads your digital book aloud. But there are rumors that Google will get into audiobooks as well)
- o iBooks

Book Distribution

Even though this is one of the most important parts of your publishing process, there are not many options available to you. Before we get into the channels through which you can distribute your books, you should have some knowledge of the subjects below:

- ISBN

    ISBN is like a social security number for your book. It captures all the relevant info for your book (title, publisher, binding, edition). Hence, if you don't have an ISBN, the chances are slim that you'll be able to sell your books, because there is no way for retailers, wholesalers, and distributors to discover them.

    Now, the question usually comes down to whether to buy your own ISBN or not.

    Here is the fact: Whoever owns the ISBN on your book is considered its publisher. Therefore, all orders and inquiries will go to them. In other words, ISBN implies control of your book, from sales to discounting to bulk sales, and more!

    Note: There are so-called "vanity publishers" out there who would use their own ISBN without even asking if you would like to purchase your own ISBN for your book. That's something you should consider before signing up with them.

- <u>Copyright Registration</u>

Here's a million-dollar question: Should you register your book with the copyright office or not? The answer is...

Yes, with copyright your work is protected the moment you create the work. Yes, it is protected when you make it commercial. And yes, registering gives you great leverage if there is infringement, where the other party has the burden to prove in court that they didn't take your work without permission.

One more thing: if any argument arises about any of the characters, as to who created him/her/it first, your dated registration proves you right (or maybe wrong).

Now the reality. No legitimate publishing company is going to go through the trouble of stealing your work. It is much easier for them to work with you to make their money. In fact, they will register your book if you have an agreement.

- <u>Print on Demand (POD)</u>

This is the heart of "today's publishing," or shall we say "self-publishing." You eliminate the upfront investment of having hundreds or maybe even thousands of books printed before your book goes on sale.

This is the aspect of modern publishing that has practically eliminated brick-and-mortar bookstores, because it opened the door to online sales without having a huge inventory at physical locations.

In a nutshell, here's how POD works:

o You have your book ready (most likely written in some type of a digital format like Microsoft Word)
o Front cover, back cover, spine are completed, and the book has gone through editing, layout, proof-reading
o You upload your book to the platform where you want it to be sold (Amazon, B&N, Smashwords, etc.)
o They approve it and publish it online
o Someone purchases a printed copy of your book
o A copy of your book is printed and sent out to the purchaser.

"No inventory, and no up-front investment are the main benefits (whereas no packaging and no mailing would be the side benefits)!"

Book Marketing and Advertising (BM&A)

This is, by far, the most important part of self-publishing! Let's face it ... hundreds, thousands of books are coming into the market each day, and you want your book to be one of them that gets read! So, how do you help people see that your book even exists?

"When you self-publish, you not only become an author, you also become a marketer and an advertiser!"

Whether you do it or hire someone else to do it for you, one way or another, marketing and advertising will have to be done, if you don't want your book getting lost among thousands of others.

Just as with other elements of self-publishing, marketing and advertising (M&A) is a huge area of the business that requires knowledge and experience. Yes, there are many books out there with titles like *How I Sold 10,000 Copies of My Book in One Month!* I wish the best of luck to those authors (but really, with just four reviews under their books??).

I'll point out that this booklet is titled *Introduction to Self-Publishing*. Please do not expect detailed information, as I intend to publish a book later in 2018 that will provide more in-depth knowledge on M&A.

Now, a brief explanation of the difference between marketing and advertising. To start with, they are not identical. Marketing entails a series of strategies that begin with determining your target audience and how you are going approach that audience and continues with setting goals for the next two years, five years—in other words, the big picture, including the tools and methods you'll use to reach your goals. Advertising is actually a part of marketing, one of the tools you use to reach the goals set in your marketing strategy. (Other tools include things like social media, press, videos, blogs, etc.)

Here are the most important parts of BM&A. Please note that each requires a good bit of knowledge to set up and run successfully. Each one also requires considerable time, sometimes even full-time attention. Nevertheless, as an author, you should be aware of their existence, do some of the work yourself, and hire a professional to do some of it for you.

> *"One way or another, as mentioned above, BM&A is the most critical part of your endeavor to become a successful self-publishing author."*

Let's have a look at some elements of BM&A briefly.

- Amazon Book Sales Strategies

    Even though the following elements are intertwined, we are going to have to split these into two.

- ## On-Page Amazon Book Sales Strategies

  This relates to work that needs to be done within the Amazon platform; it mainly depends on the following:

  o Keyword(s) you should be using in the title and subtitle of your book

  o Keyword(s) you need to use in the description of your book

  o HTML code to emphasize the keywords and other important parts of your description

  o The category (or categories) you should be in

  o The "Look inside" feature on the sales page of your book

  o The Amazon Author Page and how you should be using it

  o Advertising within the Amazon platform

  Unfortunately, Amazon does not provide any keywords or info as to which categories would bring you greater success. You need to learn, and use what you learn, to gain the experience you need to be successful at it (or hire a professional to do it for you).

- ## Off-Page Amazon Book Sales Strategies

  These are M&A methods you can use (or should use) outside the Amazon platform to direct targeted prospects to your Amazon sales page. The keyword is "*targeted*"!

  Here's what Amazon does. It keeps track of people who come to your sales page, to see what type of people buy your book. This allows their system to learn about your audience, so it can also direct people to that specific page. (Keep in mind, Amazon wants to sell, and they'll do what it takes to make a sale.) If you send highly targeted people to your book sales page and they buy your book, Amazon will learn who it should direct to your page to boost sales, and the result is increased sales of your book.

So, you have two objectives with this action:

1. Send targeted people who would be likely to buy your book to your page
2. Teach the Amazon platform what type of people would buy your book (so Amazon itself will send targeted prospects).

The question is: How do you find your targeted readers?

Some ideas:

o By setting up campaigns at book promotion sites
o Free giveaway campaigns at book promotion sites
o From your social media pages (Facebook, Twitter, etc.)
o Your author website
o Your book landing page
o Your own email campaigns (do not buy email lists—bad idea!)
o Through social media advertising campaigns
o Through Google/Bing advertising (search and display ads)

- Setting Up Campaigns at Book Promotion & Giveaway Sites

  These sites set up email campaigns and use their blogs and Facebook account to promote your book. These sites have thousands of subscribers, and mostly promote e-books. Please note that it is hard to keep up with the list of these sites, as some of them close, and some new ones open. So I will list just a few names so you can get an idea as to what they do. Seek out the current ones to find those most suitable for yourself.

- Book Pub:
  https://www.bookbub.com/partners
- Book Butterfly:
  https://www.booksbutterfly.com/
- Rafflecopter:
  https://www.rafflecopter.com/
- Book Runner:
  https://bookrunes.com/submit-book/
- You should also be aware of this: Goodreads:
  https://www.goodreads.com/giveaway

- Your Social Media Accounts

  Sounds like a no-brainer, right? Well, actually you should be aware of a few points:

  o Open an account as an author. Don't use a personal social media account where you have also posted pictures of your nephew's birthday, or the dinner you are having with friends. Be professional; this is your social media account to promote yourself as an au-thor, as well as to promote your books,

- Facebook Page is recommended rather than a standard personal Facebook account. If you don't know the difference, I recommend learning about it as soon as possible.
- Twitter is good, but it is fast. It is happening now! If you have the time to keep up with that, by all means, open an account. If your tweets are going to sit there quietly without follow up for a few weeks and your Twitter account will have only two followers, don't do it. People will find your account, and a lonely, inactive one will turn them off.
- Goodreads can be considered a social media account for authors (even though it is more than that), and it is a definite go,
- Instagram is a must. Don't be afraid of this platform; use it. Once you get the hang of it, it is much easier and a lot more social than Facebook.

- Your Author Website

  Yes, you do!

  That's the answer to the question most-asked by authors: Do I really need a website?

  And yes, you also need a blog, which you are going to update with quality content (not with news of your summer vacation!).

> **"Let's make one thing clear:**
>
> **Your website is not just a few pretty pictures put together. It is your communication channel with your readers!"**

I believe it is time to open another can of worms: SEO (Search Engine Optimization).

Just as Amazon is a world unto itself, Google is another universe—in fact, a much bigger one, and it runs on "keywords."

What are keywords? Briefly explained, they are the most-searched phrases typed into Google by users, which relate to your subject—in this case, your book(s).

The objective is to discover these keywords and implant them within your website (to start with), as well as in your M&A campaigns throughout the Internet.

To put it non-technically, the whole idea is to optimize your website with these keywords. Then start doing your M&A by using these keywords to tell Google that you are an expert on them. Once Google believes that you are the person for these keywords, your site will start rising to the first page of the Google search results.

Admittedly, that's easier said than done!

Why am I giving you all this technical stuff? Again, you should understand that your website is not just a few pictures. There is actually a science to making your website effective as a tool of your marketing and advertising. For effective SEO—Search Engine Optimization, or Internet Marketing—it may be best to ask a professional to do it for you.

- Book Landing Page

    This is an extra level of M&A! It is a single web page that contains only information about your book(s), videos, praises, testimonials, etc. You can use this page for collecting email addresses (which is one of the most important aspects of your book marketing and sales efforts.)

- Your Own Email List

    As mentioned above, collecting emails from your prospects, followers, and people who purchase books from you can help you increase the sales of your books.

    But here we're confronted with another reality: collecting emails is one thing; running email campaigns is another.

    How do you collect email addresses? Here are a few pointers:
    o From your author site
    o From your book landing page
    o Running social media campaigns
    o Running book promotions and giveaway campaigns

> *On a different note; these are the people who showed interest in your art, and you should treat them with respect.*
>
> *In other words, don't bombard them with email.*

o And how do you increase sales with these email addresses? Some things to keep in mind:

o A hard sell hardly works
o Be polite and informative: Give previews of your upcoming book
o Ask readers to do reviews. People love being a part of a good book, and good reviews mean increased sales.
o Offer discounts and signed copies if they purchase your book early.
o Be creative. These are your followers; you should know what they might be looking for, much better than anybody else.

- Social Media Advertising

Facebook is used widely for this purpose. However, depending on the genre of your book, you can also use platforms such as LinkedIn or even Tumblr to run advertising campaigns for your books.

You should keep in mind that promoting a post on Facebook is easy, but it will be most effective to use Facebook's advertising platform, which allows you to specify the demographics of your target audience, run various ads to compare which is working better, and set up separate campaigns with different objectives (e.g. directing people to your website, or to your book landing page or sales page; to garner likes; collect email addresses; download apps, etc...)

- Search and Display Ads on Google/Bing

    Search ads (or text ads) are the ones you see on the right, and at the very top, when you are doing an Internet search.

    Display ads are the image ads you see when you visit websites.

    All these ads mainly come from the two most popular search engines, Google and Bing. Just like running advertising campaigns on Facebook, you can also run your advertising campaigns by using the platforms of these two search engines.

    The name of the Google advertising platform is Adwords, and Bing's platform is Bing Ads.

- Videos

    Videos can be effective marketing and advertising tools—when done properly! You'll notice I didn't use the word "professionally," but "properly."

    It doesn't take a whole a lot of money to get a nice book video these days, unless you want to go out of your way with a professional video shoot with a cast and crew. My recommendation would be to take a look at Fiverr and paying a little extra to get a nice video made for your book, for two purposes:

1. Marketing, to share on your blog, social media, etc.
2. Advertising, to run small video campaigns on YouTube, as well as on your Facebook account.

- Press Releases

    Just like the other M&A elements, press releases should be incorporated in your book selling strategy, with the following recommendations:
    o Don't go with the free press releases, they hardly work
    o Incorporate your keywords in your press releases
    o Give a link to your website, landing page, and/or the sales page of your book
    o Include the cover illustration of your book
    o Include your photo (if possible)
    o Include a short sales-video
    o Mention your previous books
    o Mention your upcoming books
    o Pay attention to the structure of your press release (press releases have a specific structure, they are not just three to four paragraph text content written like a novel)

    Here are couple of press release distribution sites for you to start with. You can use these as a reference to find your own press release distribution company.
    Newswire: https://www.newswire.com/

    OnlinePRmedia: https://www.onlineprnews.com/

A very important point that needs to be mentioned here:

Even though these two platforms seem easy to use, be cautious when spending your hard-earned money!

They both require extensive knowledge to run effective campaigns.

Differences Between Self-Publishing and Traditional Publishing

Book Preparation Period: One of the main differences is the time it takes to publish a book. With traditional publishing, it may be years before you see your book in print. If you submit your book to a publisher, it has to go through their review and acceptance process, and it may take up to six months just to get an answer.

With self-publishing, the book can easily be completely prepared within this time period, from editing to publishing.

No Initial Investment: When you are published by a publishing company, all of the upfront investment belongs to them. Your book is locked-in by a contract for some years. But you may get some upfront money against your royalties.

When you are self-publishing, you are the publishing company. All the cost of publishing your book belongs to you. But you also take the lion's share of the sales, and your book is not locked into a contract.

Royalties: As mentioned above, you are locked into a contract for some years with a publishing company. You may get an advance, but after that the royalties are not that high—typically from 7% to 25%.

As a self-publishing author, your royalties can go up to 70%.

Corrections/Revisions: It is much easier for a self-publishing author to make corrections or revisions with the book and put the revised book back on the market in no time. This can become an arduous process in traditional publishing.

Prestige: Some authors believe that acceptance by a publisher validates their success. So yes, it is considered prestigious for an author to be signed on by a publishing house.

Book Distribution: The distribution options for a self-publishing author are as mentioned above (Amazon, B&N, Ingram, etc.) However, it is much easier for the book to get into bookstores with a publishing house.

Freedom to Choose: When your book is locked into a contract with a publisher, you are no longer in the decision-making loop. Depending on the terms of the contract, they can translate your book, sell it in a specific country but not another, and so on.

When you are a self-publishing author, the sky's the limit, as long as you are being creative enough to sell your book by any means possible. You can sell the movie rights to someone, while keeping the foreign-language rights to yourself. Or maybe you have an agent representing you in China, but you do your own sales in Australia.

Marketing & Advertising (M&A): Don't think publishers are doing all the marketing for all their authors. Increasingly, the marketing ordeal is pushed onto the authors. Some agents only want to work with authors who have an extensive mailing list.

Control Over Your Book: Once you sign a contract with a publisher, you give up on any control over elements such as the cover design, title, layout, etc.

Distribution Beyond Amazon

It's best to simply accept that Amazon is the primary place to do self-publishing. But it's not the only place to sell/distribute your books.

Here are some more places—some of them are print, some are e-book, some both, and some sell audiobooks:

Your own e-commerce site to sell e-books

iBooks

Barnes & Noble (Nook)

Kobo (Sony)

Scribd

IngramSpark

ACX

CD Baby

Feiyr

Gatekeeper Press

Google Books

Smashwords

Draft2digital

Blurb

Lulu

Tradebit

Booktango

Copyright, Distribution Rights, Exclusive/Non-Exclusive Publishing Rights

Each of these terms means something different, and as an author you should definitely know the difference.

Let's start by saying that this shouldn't be taken as legal advice; it's just a short explanation of the difference. If you have legal issues or questions, you should consult an attorney.

Furthermore, there are more rights than those mentioned here, such as movie rights, advertising rights, maybe play rights, etc. We are only going to briefly explain the big three.

Copyright

You wrote the book, you created the material, so you are the proud "*owner*" of the material, and of every single right... until you start signing contracts and making agreements.

Copyright refers to ownership of the material, and it has a few other rights attached to it that you can divide any way you like.

One little note: unless you sell the copyright (in other words, you sell the ownership of the material) it doesn't matter how you divide the other rights; you still own the material.

Having said that, there are a few points you need to be careful about! Let's continue...

Distribution Rights

This refers to where the material going to be sold, or who is going to sell it.

If you sign off on the distribution rights, that company is the only one authorized to sell your material, in any way he/she wants (and may even have the authority to decide who can or can't sell the material).

Even though you own the material, you have no way of influencing the sales of your own art.

What does that mean?

Here's a hypothetical example. Let's say you have a great book, and you gave it a nice momentum at the beginning as a self-publishing author. You know it will become an even greater book throughout the world.

You sign a distribution contract with a company that has quality distribution channels within the U.S. but does not have quality contacts abroad to properly distribute your book.

You still own your material, but it is not bringing in the income you deserve from overseas. What now?

Publishing Rights (Exclusive or Non-exclusive)

This is usually associated with royalties, and of course it also includes the distribution rights.

When you sign an exclusive publishing agreement, do you still own the copyright? Yes, you do! But during the duration of your contract, you have no say about most things. The company is the sole decision-maker for your art.

When you sign a non-exclusive publishing agreement, however, it means you can go out and find other publishing companies to work with.

Bottom Line

It is your material; you own it! You need to decide what will bring the most income to you. You can just sign one single contract to convey all your rights, or you can divide up your rights any way you want.

Suggestions

Depending on the project you are working on, publishing can be either quite simple or very complicated. Regardless, if your goal is to become a credible author, you should be focusing on your craft—your writing!

Which means you should hire professionals to do your editing, cover design, M&A, so you can concentrate on your writing. Which also means things may get expensive. Nevertheless, even though some services can get pricey, some are just a must. You should definitely have your book edited, and definitely have a Marketing & Advertising strategy to implement.

A couple of final notes:

Please don't expect to become a famous author with one book, or your first and only book. Be reasonable; the first book is usually an investment, and rarely sells thousands and thousands of copies right off the bat.

If you are going to invest in Marketing & Advertising, make sure you have more books in the works.

www.ingramcontent.com/pod-product-compliance
Lightning Source LLC
Chambersburg PA
CBHW060646280326
41933CB00012B/2180